*L*ife comes at us like a bullet these days—fast…unforgiving. But these times are full of amazing possibilities for people who rise to the occasion.

The pressing challenge is to get better, quicker.

This new era demands more rapid responses. Immediate adaptability. Fast results. Above all, it requires a personal growth rate that at least can match the growing pace of change.

We must speed up our adjustments to frequent career shifts and new work roles. We must find a formula that helps us pull far more of our raw potential into play. We must figure out how to make a contribution that really counts. Only by applying ourselves differently can we deliver the kind of outcomes the world has come to expect.

The skill sets that made us successful last year can leave us defenseless tomorrow. The education we thought we'd "completed" soon quits protecting our careers. Even a good base of experience provides little safety, because it so easily becomes outdated.

Deep inside, we know something more is needed now.

The situation calls for a powerful new strategy. We need a methodology for rapidly mobilizing ourselves to measure up against the career flash points we constantly encounter.

The secret is *accelerated personal growth*…a deliberate, disciplined routine that produces dramatic performance gains.

Follow the guidelines given in this handbook, and you'll push your personal effectiveness to all-time highs.

PRITCHETT & ASSOCIATES, INC.

PRICE PRITCHETT

A Career Acceleration Strategy

Fas

rowth

A Career Acceleration Strategy

Invest heavily in the *now.*

Fast growth requires a keen awareness of what you're doing with yourself. You need a strong sense of "now-ness." Or to put it another way, it's important for you to maximize the value of the moment.

Time is one of your most precious resources, and you don't get a second chance to use it. Your first shot is your last one. No do-overs. You only get one crack at using any given time period for performance improvement.

So pay attention. Consciously watch how you're spending the fleeting now, and consider the payback you'll get. Are you making a good investment of your hours and minutes? Or are you wasting these scarce resources…spending time on stuff that offers little return…fumbling the opportunity for fast growth?

By the way, this is a far bigger issue than it used to be. Speed can be more important for your success than twenty more IQ points might be.

The slower you go in developing yourself today, the faster you'll need to move tomorrow. Today's world refuses to wait on anyone. We must learn to grow more rapidly, or we'll fall further and further behind. We need to accelerate our adaptability because change keeps picking up speed.

And let's not kid ourselves—this is a *personal* problem. It belongs to each of us, privately, as individuals. Nobody can fix it for us. We can't delegate our use of the now to someone else. We own it—completely.

Of course, this means each person is in a position to handle the situation. You're in control. You can do something. You're the one living your life, and you can choose to live it more powerfully.

Just remember, growth can only occur in the present. So you need to show a high respect for *now.* Fill it with the right behaviors, and you'll be rewarded with fast results.

"I was in the drug store the other day
trying to get a cold medication…
Not easy.
There's an entire wall of products that you need.
You stand there going,
'Well, this one is quick acting but this is long lasting…
Which is more important, the present or the future?'"

– Jerry Seinfeld

"Once upon a time, you could live in three tenses—the past, the present, and the future. There was time to consult history; there was time to plan for what lay ahead.

The present tense was spent managing the transfer of the past into the future and imagining what that future might be. Today, under the pressure of accelerating change, the past and future have been fused into a single tense: the present.

The present is real time
and real time is the only time."

–Jim Taylor and Watts Wacker, with Howard Means,
The 500 Year Delta

Grow toward the sun.

Plants aim themselves at sunlight, and they do it for a good reason. It helps them grow. Likewise, you need to "align with the universe." Fast results come easier and count for more when you grow in the direction the world wants you to go.

Your self-development efforts should be aimed at building competencies somebody really wants to buy. In this case, we're talking about your employer, the outfit that pays for your services. That's *your* customer. Your sunshine. So point yourself toward those rays. Basically this means growing in ways that will bring an employer the key benefit: new profits.

Fast growth in the career sense doesn't automatically come from making *yourself* better. It comes from being able to benefit your employer better. Having "talent" is not the issue—the question is can you deliver as a powerful profit-improver? And it's not enough to be a nice, high-quality person—ask yourself if you're an all-star at adding value.

Now don't take this wrong. We're not discounting the importance of integrity, character, attitude and such. We're not saying talent doesn't matter. But the reality is that employers don't really care how good you are per se. What they truly care about is how good you will make *them*.

This may sound cold. Or too commercial. But it will help you focus your efforts on *relevant* growth.

Concentrate on developing yourself in ways that will bring superior value to the end user of you. Make sure you know and respect your employer's needs. Emphasize how you as a human being can add value to the organization that's hiring you, and you create high market value for yourself.

If you develop yourself in the right direction, you can put a premium price tag on yourself and still be seen as a bargain. Contribute enough,

5

and you'll create high demand for your work.

Like it or not, every one of us is at the mercy of the market. We'll be most successful at building our careers if we always remember to grow and sell what that market wants to buy.

"I was a vegetarian until
I started leaning toward the sunlight."

– Rita Rudner

Employment in the future
will be characterized by micro-careers.

People will find themselves in constantly shifting
assignments. We'll work on short-lived projects,
with changing sets of co-workers, in fluctuating
roles that require new competencies.

micro-careers

So here's the 21st century challenge:
How quickly can you ramp up, re-tool yourself
and produce results that add major value?

Trust in the power of *future pull.*

You can grow at a faster clip if you'll put the future to work for you. Tomorrow is your ally.

The key is to let the future know specifically what you want from it. Start by coming up with a clear mental picture of your goal. Keep it alive in your mind. Visit it often in your imagination. The future will start organizing events to help bring about this thing you want.

Most people don't appreciate how this technique can accelerate a person's growth and accomplishments. Maybe it hits you as just too vague. Or you don't give it a shot because you can't figure out *why* it should work. The truth is, it may sound too simplistic for you to take it seriously.

But this isn't baloney. The great psychologist, Alfred Adler, emphasized the "teleological" power of goals. By this he meant how goals or purpose seem to shape natural processes or events. He argued that goals somehow help create the conditions needed for their fulfillment.

Is this getting too heavy for you? Stay with me here—this is a far more potent idea than you might imagine. Don't dismiss it just because you think it's a little random.

Arthur Kostler states, "The pull of the future is as real as the pressure of the past." And author George Land writes that the future may play a more important role than our past in causing us to be where and what we are.

Their point? The future shapes us. It carries major influence over our *becoming*.

But you can influence how the future influences you. Chart a certain course for yourself, and you tell the future how it's supposed to help you. Your personal vision of what you want to become instructs the future on how to provide assistance. Your mental picture of what you hope to achieve tells tomorrow how to help. Just set the goal. Its magnetic power will pull you toward its realization.

Here's the rub—the future can't help you if you don't know what you want. You have to pick your aiming point. Unless you deliberately set the direction for yourself, the future doesn't know which way to pull.

So like a catchy book title says, "If you don't know where you're going, you'll probably end up somewhere else."

"I went into a general store.
They wouldn't let me buy
anything specifically."

– *Steven Wright*

The future behaves differently
than it used to.
It comes at us faster now,
and affects us more powerfully
than before.

Just as a 75 mile per hour wind isn't
three times as forceful as a 25 mile per
hour wind—but instead is *nine times
more powerful*—the accelerating future
will surprise us with the speed and impact
that mark its arrival.

We must learn how to turn
its power to our advantage.

ture

Be sharply pointed rather than well rounded.

You can't do everything fast. So you have to figure out where speed will count the most. Decide where your growth can make the biggest difference, then drive hard in that direction.

Fast growth is a sacrificial act. To pull it off, you have to steal from other areas of your life. Something has to give over here in order for you to grow over there. We're talking about significant tradeoffs. Serious compromises. A hard-fisted rationing of resources, such as your time, energy and attention span.

Don't try out for the fast growth game if your top priority is a so-called well-balanced life. You're going to have to whittle down, sharpen your focus, narrow yourself—all this so you can give more to fewer efforts.

Fast growth is greedy. It takes a lot to feed the beast. And why take food off other plates to satisfy this creature's appetite? Because this is the beast you're betting on to protect your future.

Besides, some of the stuff that's been eating up your time and energy deserves to starve. It's all the clutter you've let creep into your life that really doesn't contribute anything to your future. It's the diddley routines you follow out of habit. And it's the urgent but trivial gunk that nags at you for attention, yet gives you nothing to help you grow. Now's the time to kick these beggars away from the table.

Think few. Concentrate on the essentials. Figure out what to ignore.

We actually have *too many choices* available to us, and this seriously complicates our time management. It also causes stress and stunts our development. To speed our growth we must simplify. What this comes down to is deliberately managing choices out of our lives.

Instead of scattering yourself, responding freely to the odds and ends that swarm around you, decide what really counts. Downsize your daily activities. Don't blunt your personal development by trying to do too many things at once. Only by sharply focusing yourself can you achieve the critical mass of energy required for real acceleration.

The fuel for fast growth comes when energy is *contained...
compressed...channeled*. It's simply a matter of giving yourself more
fully on a more narrow front. Power accumulates quickly when there
are fewer ways for it to escape.

"Things that matter most
must never be at the mercy
of things that matter least."

– Johann Wolfgang von Goethe

Focus actually frees up time.
Rather than consuming a person, it liberates.
Instead of stretching us thinner,
focus keeps us from overextending ourselves.

Selectivity in how we spend our time
enables us to allocate more hours and days to
those few things that count the most to us.

Narrow life down to what's precious
and necessary. In a world of complexity,
the best weapon is simplicity.

Create white space, then innovate.

The kind of growth we're looking for here often comes from stopping more than speeding up. You can only accelerate your learning and development so much by simply doing the same old things faster. Sooner or later you must start doing different things.

Quitting plays a key role in the process of rapid growth. You'll need to break some familiar rhythms, actually *unlearn* things and find more effective performance strategies.

What this comes down to is destabilizing yourself, and doing it on purpose. We're not talking about a minor tweaking of the way you typically do things either. Fast growth occurs through transformation. It's more like a metamorphosis, a major shift that enables you to move to a higher plain of performance. This is breakthrough behavior, and it's based on abandoning old approaches.

Don't let this spook you. You've done it many times before. Like when you stopped crawling and started walking. Think back. You didn't crawl so fast that you came up off all fours and began walking. It wasn't a matter of raw speed and momentum that put you on your feet. And when you went from wading to swimming...that didn't occur because you managed to wade water so quickly. You made the shift to swimming by giving up on wading and engaging new moves.

When you stopped crawling and wading, you created some white space for yourself. Some real growing room. And you filled that space with purposeful experimentation. You knew what you wanted, and took new risks. You were innovative. You were an adventurer, an explorer, you found new potential within yourself.

Give yourself permission to play with life that way again.

Start by stopping. Actually, this is probably the hardest part of all. Giving up old habits and thought patterns—the unlearning—is tough for people to do. But old approaches get in the way of trying out new methods. You can't crawl and walk at the same time. You can't keep

17

wading if you want to swim. Something has to give.

The second step in the breakthrough process is experimentation. Tryouts. And the big requirement here is a willingness to fail. Mistakes guide you toward your goal, and you won't get far without making them. These bumps and bruises are very educational. They belong in the process.

Fast growth will feel like it did when you were learning to ride a bike. Remember? You got banged up a little. You came out of it with scrapes and scratches. But you mastered the bike, and the huge grin on your face offered proof that you'd made another breakthrough.

Shoot for fast growth, and give yourself a chance to grin like that again.

"We make ourselves up as we go."

– *Kate Green*

We've experienced profound shifts
in two major dimensions—space and time.

Just think—you as a human being
can travel to any place on planet earth
in less than 24 hours. And you now can move
information anywhere at the speed of light—
186,300 miles per second—the fastest
speed known to mankind.

Distance doesn't matter like it used to. And the accelerating pace of change causes tremendous compression of time.

What this means is that we must do more than change—*we must change the way we change.*

Learn on the fly.

Growth doesn't get started until you do. You must move…take action…mobilize yourself.

Sounds easy enough on the surface. But people get paralyzed by "planning." They freeze up getting "prepared" to grow. Seems we want to figure out the answer before we start working on the problem. We like to do our learning first, then put it into action.

Fast growth calls for a more freewheeling approach. You must operate on the basis of learning *as* you go, not *before* you go.

"Getting ready" often gives a person the feeling of progress, but it's usually a delaying tactic that gets in the way of growth. "Getting going" is what puts you further down the road. As Mack Hanan, author of *Fast-Growth Management*, states, "The main growth strategy is the willingness to move."

If you want to see how this works, just plop a kid down in front of a computer. Or behind the wheel of a car. The youngster has little patience for "learning" before getting started. Kids just want to go for it. They use an action-based strategy of learning as they go. And that enables them to master the machine a lot quicker than most adults who also are starting from scratch.

Active pursuit of your personal development goals provides a steady stream of feedback. Actually doing things—trying out different approaches—gives you hard data on what works and what doesn't. Mobility is the secret. Constant movement keeps you supplied with fresh answers. Forward motion feeds you new insights.

Of course, allowing yourself to learn on the fly carries a price: You must also become more willing to make mistakes. More trials mean you can expect more errors. Going forward before you have everything figured out guarantees a higher failure rate.

The payoff comes in the rapid learning curve. Forward motion offers the fastest education you can find.

"Instead of having 'answers' on a math test,
they should just call them 'impressions,'
and if you got a different 'impression,'
so what, can't we all be brothers?"

– *Jack Handy,* Deep Thoughts

Our word career comes from the French word carrière, which originally meant "a racing course." As a verb, it means "to move at full speed."

In today's world, careering comes down to a race against change... a personal contest to see if we can grow as fast as the challenges we face in our work.

Our schooling needs to move
at full speed, and this calls for
a strategy of "learning in motion."

Benchmark.

How rapidly would your results improve if, starting today, you did what the highest performers do?

You can take a lot of the mystery out of personal growth simply by studying people who are great examples. Find some folks that you'd call "best in class." Carefully observe their behavior—watch what they do...how they go about it...the fine points of their approach. Then, once you've sorted out how they do things differently from you, start copying their techniques.

Pretty straightforward, wouldn't you say?

It's an obvious way to go about building a better you. But most people fail to do it in a deliberate, disciplined fashion. Instead of analyzing the most successful individuals and adopting their moves, we grind along trying to get better at our own way of doing things.

Fast growth comes much easier when we rely on role models to guide our actions. Their methods can serve as a shortcut. They offer visible proof of what's possible, and how to pull it off.

Why don't we use this benchmarking routine more often?

Maybe it's because we believe the top performers are just blessed with more potential than we personally have to work with. But the people who set the standards—the highest achievers—aren't necessarily the brightest or the ones with the most pure talent. Sometimes they've just developed a better formula—they do things differently, and it delivers a lot better results. Sure, brainpower helps. And no question, innate ability gives a person an advantage. Still, all of us can think of plenty examples where we've seen talented people outperformed by others who actually have less potential.

Start practicing the moves of the people you admire the most, and see what happens. Keep analyzing how they operate. Keep comparing it to the way you go about doing things. If their performance really does represent "best practices," it's probably the result of several factors, including attitude and work habits as well as basic skills. That's all part of the performance package. Watch for the subtleties, and weave them into your repertoire.

Benchmarking is all about imitating the best. But it doesn't mean you have to sacrifice your individuality. You'll still have plenty of room for your own personality to show. It'll just shine through more powerfully than ever before.

"We've been working on the basics because,
basically,
we've been having trouble with the basics."

– Bob Ojeda, L.A. Dodgers pitcher

Somebody knows how to do it better.

Get close enough to watch.
That puts you in the schoolroom.

Then just do what you did when
you were first learning how to learn…
when your personal growth was the fastest
it's ever been. Study the other person's
technique. Mimic those moves.
Make more attempts, more tryouts.

That's how you learned to walk when you were
a mere infant. And how you mastered a language
in a matter of months…from scratch.

"Stretch out" when resistance hits.

When you push yourself to grow in a hurry, you hit yourself where it hurts: right smack in your habits. You start interfering with familiar routines. You disturb the comfortable patterns in the way you live your life. Before long, something deep inside starts pushing back.

These are the moments of truth. You're about to find out how much you *really* want fast growth.

The biggest challenge to overcome will be these negative reactions— your own resistance to change. Human nature being what it is, a part of you will fight hard to keep you pretty much the way you are.

You should get to know this enemy within. Understand how resistance operates. Expect it to attack, and learn how to conquer it. Otherwise, your growth efforts are likely to fizzle out far short of what you hope for as resistance overcomes your ambitions.

You might as well start out expecting to cause trouble for yourself. As soon as you kick off your fast growth efforts, resistance will probably rear its ugly head. The first step toward overcoming it is not to let it take you by surprise. Just as you would expect to feel stiff and sore if you began a new exercise routine, count on feeling uncomfortable with your beginning efforts at fast growth.

Resistance is a great con artist. It tries to make you believe that sticking with your growth plans will be too painful. Too difficult. Not worth the struggle. It wants to sweet talk you into selling out your future for a little immediate comfort. But just like stretching out and continuing your physical exercise helps you work out muscle soreness, hanging in there with your fast growth program pushes you past the resistance.

Remember this very important point—resistance grows stronger with any evidence of weakening resolve, but it yields to renewed effort. So the best thing you can do to conquer the enemy is meet it head-on. Stretch yourself a bit more. Push for still faster growth.

29

This is psychological warfare at its best, and it will keep your ambitions alive.

"If you start to take Vienna, take Vienna."

– Napoleon Bonaparte

The fastest way to build muscle is through "resistance exercises." Like weightlifting, for example. Muscles actually need that kind of effort or work in order to grow.

Try to "protect" your muscles from resistance, and they begin to shrink. You get weaker.

owth

Resistance is how your insides tell you
something unusual is going on.
Don't misinterpret the message.
It's simply a signal that you're
at the edge of growth.

Be gutsy in how you begin.

Start your growth program with bold strokes. Courageous acts. Your opening moves should be strong enough to overcome inertia, give you instant momentum and create excitement inside.

Audacious action energizes a person. It's like the initial thrust a rocket needs to clear the launch pad. Gutsy moves will power you forward, enabling you to escape the gravity field that pulls you back toward your same old daily patterns.

New habits are not easy to come by, and old habits are even tougher to break. You need to hit hard. Fracture your routines. Shatter the status quo in how you've been growing and developing as a person.

William James, who's called "the father of American psychology," said there are three rules to follow if you want to change your life: (1) Start immediately. (2) Do it flamboyantly. (3) No exceptions. These recommendations produce a sense of urgency, an air of drama, and the level of commitment you'll need for fast growth.

Bold moves in the way you begin mean you'll have to invest more of yourself. You'll be gambling a bigger amount from the very outset. And that's good. That goes a long way toward keeping you in the game. A person is less likely to call it quits if it means leaving a lot on the table.

If you open boldly enough, it's sort of like "burning your boats." You have to stick it out and try your best to win the war, because you've cut off your escape routes. What it amounts to is putting yourself in a position where you're more or less forced to grow. You're cornered by your courageous acts, and now you have to rise to the occasion.

Robert Frey stated in a *Harvard Business Review* article, "The people who change best and fastest are the ones who have no choice." So start big. The way you begin says a lot about how you'll finish.

Fast growth shouldn't start slow.

"You fought the good fight.
You were in it right up to the beginning."

– Bruce Babbitt, Secretary of the Interior

draw first

Draw first.

Shoot high.

Leverage your big winner behaviors.

Let's apply the *Pareto Principle*—what's known as "the 80-20 rule"—to your fast growth program.

The argument goes like this: 80 percent of your performance gains will come from 20 percent of your growth efforts. Once again, what we're saying is that a few critical behaviors will account for most of your fast growth. The biggest part of your efforts—say about 80 percent—will be so much less effective that they'll produce only 20 percent of your improvement.

It's peculiar how things just seem to pan out this way if we let nature take its course. We spread our energies around, investing in a variety of activities that seem worthwhile. But our return on investment varies dramatically from one set of behaviors to another. A few efforts, aimed at a few particular goals, end up making the major contributions to our personal growth.

Just think how much you can accelerate your growth by allocating your personal resources more carefully. Spend your time, energy and attention in the high-payoff areas, and you could easily double or triple your speed in personal development.

Fast growth comes from disproportionate investment. That is, it happens when you focus on big winner behaviors...when you're unfair in the way you distribute your efforts and resources.

You won't get great results simply by staying busy. Or being responsible. Or even by trying hard and turning out pretty good work. It's not effort or activity that counts, but *outcomes*. You have to examine your productive hours, and identify what it is that seems to drive your development the most. In particular, what do you do that contributes the most to fast growth?

These are the power points. They deserve the lion's share of your productive hours and energy, because they'll bring you the best returns.

If you want maximum rewards, don't make the mistake of seeking "balance" in your workday routine. Instead, rely heavily on the big winner behaviors to leverage your growth rate.

"Our strength
is that we don't have any weaknesses.
Our weakness
is that we don't have any real strengths."

*–Frank Broyles, University of Arkansas football coach,
on the team's prospects*

"A typical pattern will show that 80 percent of outputs result from 20 percent of inputs; that 80 percent of consequences flow from 20 percent of causes; or that 80 percent of results come from 20 percent of effort.

A few things are important; most are not.

The few things that work fantastically well should be identified, cultivated, nurtured and multiplied. At the same time, the waste—the majority of things that will always prove to be of low value to man and beast—should be abandoned or severely cut back."

– *Richard Koch,* The 80/20 Principle

Build a power grid of relationships.

Fast growth is not a one-person show. Other people play a key role in the process. In fact, your speed and overall success in developing yourself will depend heavily on the ability to make quick and lasting connections with others.

The faster you want to grow, the more you'll need support systems...contacts...key relationships. Other people are in control of opportunities. They can open doors, offer know-how, and help you through the rough spots.

Technical skills will take you only so far, and they're not enough to keep you on the fast track. You also need to become an expert at meeting and getting along with people.

We live today in an interconnected world, and that highlights the importance of interpersonal skills. If you're good at networking, you've got an advantage. Business has gotten big on teamwork. Partnering. Alliances and joint venturing. To position yourself for maximum growth, you need to excel at relationship management.

Put a very high priority on building a power grid of relationships. Then protect it. Keep strengthening the strands, tightening the connections, even as you add others to the network. "Who you know" has always been important. But it will become an even bigger success factor in the future.

Make a habit of taking the initiative in social situations. First determine whom it makes sense to spend time with, and engineer those encounters. The idea is to create a circle of valuable contacts, people who have the potential to contribute to your personal growth. Reach out. Connect quickly. Then cultivate the relationship—keep it alive by making it worthwhile and pleasing to the other person.

Build a reputation for being a giver, so others end up wanting to reciprocate. The idea is to create a positive bank account with people—a store of good will—so you're never in debt if you go asking for favors. Make sure others have solid reasons for wanting to help you succeed.

Shooting for fast growth is a lonely, futile struggle unless you can enlist the help of others. And the best way to win their backing is for *you* to help *them* succeed.

"My mother used to say
there are no strangers,
only friends you haven't yet met.
She's now in a maximum security
twilight home in Australia."

– *Dame Edna Everage*

In the past, organizations strategized
to gain *competitive advantage*. The emphasis in
the future will be to gain *cooperative* advantage.

conne

More and more, our interconnected world
requires—and rewards—those who are skilled
in the connection process.

A core competency needed in individuals and organizations alike is connectivity.

A core competency needed in individuals and organizations alike is connectivity.

A core competency needed in individuals and organizations alike is connectivity.

A core competency needed in individuals and organizations alike is connectivity.

A core competency needed in individuals and organizations alike is connectivity.

A core competency needed in individuals and organizations alike is connectivity.

ctivity

A core competency needed in individuals and organizations alike is connectivity.

Use it or lose it.

The pace of growth picks up when you start engaging yourself more fully. Using your talents to a greater degree doesn't use them up. In fact, personal resources actually multiply the more you put them to work.

This is the physics of fast growth. You can look at it as a law of increasing returns: The more you use your talents and personal resources, the more you have to use.

But this law is a knife that cuts both ways. To the extent that we fail to use our talents, energy, opportunities and such, the gods take them away. We lose what we don't use.

What this says to us is that we can't "save up" these resources. If you hoard them, hoping to keep them safely in some personal storehouse for your future use, they won't grow. Instead they start to decay. Your potential shrinks when it's not employed. But the minute you make it go to work, it begins to expand.

You've heard the old saying, "You have to spend money to make money." Likewise, you must use muscle to make muscle...or plant seeds if you want to grow more seeds. The biblical parable of the talents reveals these natural dynamics at work. It gives a philosophy for fast growth, and argues in favor of fully utilizing yourself. Work on growing, and the easier it gets to grow. Develop yourself faster, and you'll find it increasingly easy to accelerate your development even more.

What this means is that your growth rate can be measured as a function of how effectively you are putting your resources to use. You could almost make this into a mathematical equation. Feel like you're not growing? This says you're not spending your talents, that you're sitting on your potential instead of putting it to work.

Want more out of yourself? Is there some aspect you wish to change and improve? Use it. Invest it. Spend it. Do *something* with it, otherwise it gradually diminishes. That's because you just can't put personal growth on hold. If you decide to wait, you have less to work with when you actually do begin. So the sooner you start, the better.

You're blessed with many personal gifts that can greatly speed up your growth. It's time to open them. Enjoy them. Put them to good use—*now*—so that they can begin to expand. According to the law of increasing returns, the more you use, the more you have.

"I discovered you never know yourself until you're tested and that you don't even know you're being tested until afterwards, and that in fact there isn't anyone giving the test except yourself."

– *Marilyn French*, The Bleeding Heart

Books By Price Pritchett

* *Fast Growth: A Career Acceleration Strategy*

* *Outsourced: The Employee Handbook—12 New Rules for Running Your Career in an Interconnected World*

  Mindshift: The Employee Handbook for Understanding the Changing World of Work

* *New Work Habits for a Radically Changing World*

* *Firing Up Commitment During Organizational Change*

  Resistance: Moving Beyond the Barriers to Change

* *Business As UnUsual: The Handbook for Managing and Supervising Organizational Change* (Co-authored with Ron Pound)

* *The Employee Handbook for Organizational Change* (Co-authored with Ron Pound)

* *Team ReConstruction: Building a High Performance Work Group During Change* (Co-authored with Ron Pound)

* *Teamwork: The Team Member Handbook*

* *High-Velocity Culture Change: A Handbook for Managers* (Co-authored with Ron Pound)

* *Culture Shift: The Employee Handbook for Changing Corporate Culture*

  The Ethics of Excellence

  A Survival Guide to the Stress of Organizational Change (Co-authored with Ron Pound)

* *Service Excellence!*

  Smart Moves: A Crash Course on Merger Integration Management (Co-authored with Ron Pound)

* *Mergers: Growth in the Fast Lane* (Co-authored with Robert D. Gilbreath)

  The Employee Survival Guide to Mergers and Acquisitions

  After the Merger: The Authoritative Guide for Integration Success

  Making Mergers Work: A Guide to Managing Mergers and Acquisitions

  The Quantum Leap Strategy

  you²: A High-Velocity Formula for Multiplying Your Personal Effectiveness in Quantum Leaps

---

* Training program also available. Please call 1-800-992-5922 for more information.
Call 972-789-7999 for information regarding international rights and foreign translations.

O R D E R   F O R M

Fast Growth

A Career Acceleration Strategy

1-99 copies	_____ copies at $6.95 each
100-999 copies	_____ copies at $6.75 each
1,000-4,999 copies	_____ copies at $6.50 each
5,000-9,999 copies	_____ copies at $6.25 each
10,000 or more copies	_____ copies at $6.00 each

Name _____

Job Title _____

Organization _____

Phone _____

Street Address _____

P.O. Box _____

City, State _____ Zip _____

Country _____

Purchase order number (if applicable) _____

E-mail address _____

Applicable sales tax, shipping and handling charges will be added. Prices subject to change.

Orders less than $100 require prepayment. $100 or more may be invoiced.

☐ Check Enclosed   ☐ Please Invoice

☐ **VISA**   ☐ **MasterCard**   ☐ **AMERICAN EXPRESS**

Account Number _____ Expiration Date _____

Signature _____

To order, call: **800-992-5922**

fax: **972-789-7900**
e-mail: http://www.PritchettNet.com/order
or mail this form to the address below

Pritchett & Associates, Inc.

13155 Noel Road, Suite 1600, Dallas, Texas 75240
http://www.PritchettNet.com

EJ7498

Fast Growth Training Program

This workshop teaches people to win by—

- **Aligning personal goals with organizational objectives**
- **Adapting to change**
- **Adding value to all shareholders in the process**

It provides a breakthrough strategy for accelerated personal growth, and that creates a new pathway to organizational growth.

The program helps individuals formulate a Personal Growth Strategy which ensures career acceleration, competency and employability. Participants learn how to channel their talent and creativity into tangible organizational outcomes.

With *Fast Growth* training, organizations tap into the most valuable asset they possess—their people.

For more information about this training program, call 1-800-992-5922.

Pritchett & Associates Consulting Services

Today's marketplace calls for bold strategies. Audacious plans. This may mean mergers and acquisitions. Outsourcing. Alliances/joint ventures. Or some other organizational transformation aimed at fast growth.

Strategy Deployment

Pritchett & Associates has over two decades of experience helping organizations translate high-powered plans into hard results. To start with, we make sure you come off the line fast. Our consultants help you craft and execute those all-important opening moves. But mobilizing your organization is only the beginning. Our job is to help you maintain momentum, and to ensure the alignment necessary to keep your strategy execution on track.

A Focus on Hard Results

From the kickoff, through the "messy middle" of the change process, all the way to the wrap-up stage of strategy implementation, Pritchett & Associates' consultants keep an acute focus on the commercial aspects of your organization. On productivity. Profitability. Quality. Customer service.

We help you create a well-orchestrated, wall-to-wall crusade so you can capture today's opportunities before they escape.

If you would like to talk to one of our consultants about your unique organizational challenges, please call us at 1-888-852-1250

Price Pritchett is Chairman and CEO of
Pritchett & Associates, Inc., a Dallas-based firm
specializing in mergers, outsourcing and
organizational change. He has authored over
20 books on individual and organizational
performance, and is recognized internationally
as a leading authority on the dynamics of
change. He holds a Ph.D. in psychology and
has consulted to top executives in major
corporations for over two decades.